Spirits of the Frontier

True Tales of the Paranormal in the Wild West

By Lee Brickley

Spectral Cowboys: The Ghosts of Dead Man's Hole..............109

The Haunting Melodies of the Ghost Dancer.......................115

The Phantom Prospector of Death Valley..............................121

El Paso's Haunted Hotel: The De Soto....................................125

The Crying Ghost of La Llorona in New Mexico...................131

Bigfoot of the Rockies: Myth or Reality?...............................137

Specter of Hangman's Bridge: Justice or Vengeance?.........143

UFOs over Aurora: The 1897 Crash..151

Legends of the Lake: The Spirits of Pyramid Lake...............157

Afterword..163

About The Author..167

Introduction

The American West has always been a land of mystery, a place where the unknown and the inexplicable have found a home amid vast plains, towering mountains, and windswept deserts. For as long as humans have ventured into these territories, stories have lingered—tales of ghosts, curses, creatures, and unexplained phenomena that have challenged our understanding of the world. My name is Lee Brickley, and I have dedicated my life to unravelling the truth behind these supernatural enigmas.

My journey into the paranormal began in my youth. A fascination with the unexplainable led me to delve into history, folklore, and the scientific study of phenomena beyond ordinary comprehension. Over time, I realised that my passion was not just a hobby but a calling. I became a paranormal investigator, probing into the shadows and unearthing stories that many would prefer to keep buried.

It has been a pursuit filled with wonder, fear, disbelief, and discovery, leading me down paths I never could have imagined.

The Wild West has always held a particular allure for me. It is a time and place where reality and legend intertwine, where the boundaries between the natural and supernatural blur. In this era of pioneers and prospectors, lawmen and outlaws, the human spirit was tested by a harsh and unforgiving landscape. And yet, amid the struggles and triumphs, there emerged tales of the paranormal that have endured to this day. These stories are not mere fabrications or products of overactive imaginations. They are part of the very fabric of American history, a testament to the complex interplay between our physical world and the realms beyond.

In "Spirits of the Frontier: True Tales of the Paranormal in the Wild West," we will embark on a journey through 25 stand-alone chapters, each focusing on a different true paranormal encounter or event from the wild west days. This is not a work of fiction or a collection of embellished legends. It is a serious and rigorous exploration of the supernatural, grounded in historical research, eyewitness accounts, and, where possible, scientific investigation.

We'll venture into the ghost towns and haunted hotels where spectral residents refuse to leave. We'll explore the cursed mines and mystical mountains where treasures are guarded by otherworldly forces. We'll meet the ghostly cowboys, phantom stagecoaches, mysterious witches, and elusive creatures that inhabit the folklore of the American West. And along the way, we'll uncover truths that challenge our understanding of reality.

The Wild West is a symbol of a time when the rules were not yet fully written, where the known world was expanding, and where anything seemed possible. It's a time that still resonates with us, and it's no wonder that it has given birth to some of the most compelling paranormal stories in our nation's history. As we dig into these tales, we'll not only delve into the supernatural but also into the human condition, exploring themes of greed, love, ambition, fear, and the eternal quest for understanding.

Each chapter in this book is a self-contained story, allowing you to explore the paranormal landscape at your own pace. Some tales may be familiar, while others may be entirely new. Yet, they all share a common thread: they are glimpses into a world that exists just beyond our ordinary perception, a world that beckons and bewilders, frightens, and fascinates.

My goal is not merely to entertain but to enlighten. As a paranormal investigator, I have learned to approach each case with an open mind and a critical eye. I strive to separate fact from fiction, reality from illusion, truth from legend. In this book, I present to you my findings, laid bare and unfiltered. I invite you to join me in this exploration, to question and to seek, to ponder and to wonder.

For those of you who are new to the paranormal, I welcome you to a realm of infinite possibilities. For those well-versed in the supernatural, I challenge you to look deeper and to see the familiar in a new light. Together, we will walk the line between the known and the unknown, guided by curiosity, courage, and a desire to comprehend the incomprehensible.

The wild west days may be long gone, but the spirits of the frontier are still with us. They linger in the shadows, whispering secrets and waiting for those brave enough to listen. This book is an invitation to hear their voices, to step into their world, and to glimpse the mysteries that have shaped our nation's history.

Join me, dear reader, as we venture into the unknown, where the past is never truly dead, and where the spirits of the frontier continue to beckon us from beyond.

Yours in discovery,

Lee Brickley

The Ghost of Tombstone:

Wyatt Earp's Haunting

In the raw, wild stretches of the American Southwest, where the sun scorches the earth and the wind carries whispers of a time long past, there lies the small, enigmatic town of Tombstone, Arizona. A town frozen in time, where echoes of gunshots still ring in the air, and legends of the Wild West continue to thrive. Among those legends, none is more haunting, more enduring, than the ghost of Wyatt Earp.

Wyatt Berry Stapp Earp, one of the most iconic figures of the Western frontier, left an indelible mark on Tombstone. His life was a tapestry of contradictions, woven with threads of law, violence, gambling, and a relentless pursuit of justice. A man of both virtue and vice, Wyatt Earp's complex character makes him a fitting subject for a spectral dead and several wounded, embedding Wyatt Earp in the annals of Western lore.

But Earp's story did not end there. The gunfight led to further violence and vendetta, as both sides sought revenge. Earp's younger brother, Morgan, was killed, and another brother, Virgil, was crippled. Wyatt's response was a bloody vendetta ride, during which he hunted down and killed those he believed responsible for his family's suffering.

Such was the nature of Wyatt Earp's existence in Tombstone: a turbulent mix of law and lawlessness, love and hate, triumph and tragedy. A life so full of conflict and emotion, it is little wonder that his spirit is said to linger, restless and unresolved.

But there is another dimension to the haunting, one that transcends mere sightings and sensations. It is the idea that Wyatt Earp's ghost has assumed a protective role over Tombstone. Many accounts suggest that his spectral presence serves as a guardian, intervening in times of trouble, maintaining order, and upholding the law from beyond the grave.

Is there truth to this legend? Can a spirit retain its earthly role, acting as a sentinel over a place and its people? Or is this simply a romantic notion, a way for the town to preserve its connection to a figure so central to its identity?

There is no definitive answer. Ghosts, by their very nature, dwell in the realm of the unknown, the unexplainable. They challenge our understanding of reality, urging us to look beyond the material world, to consider possibilities that defy logic and reason.

The haunting of Wyatt Earp in Tombstone, Arizona, is such a phenomenon. It is a tale rich with history, emotion, and mystery. A tale that invites us to explore the human soul, the nature of memory, and the power of legend. A tale that reminds us that the past is never truly gone, that it lingers in the shadows, waiting for the opportune moment to make itself known.

So, if you ever find yourself in Tombstone, walking the dusty streets that Wyatt Earp once tread, be mindful of the wind that rustles the leaves, the creaking of old wooden doors, the fleeting shadow in the corner of your eye. For you may just encounter a piece of history, a glimpse of a time when the frontier was wild, and the line between the living and the dead was but a thin veil, easily crossed.

And as the sun dips below the horizon, casting an orange glow over the desert, you may hear the faint jingle of spurs, the soft whisper of a voice that refuses to be silenced. Wyatt Earp's ghost, forever a part of Tombstone, forever a reminder of the spirits of the frontier.

The Nevada Triangle: Disappearances and Mysteries

A land of rugged mountains, expansive deserts, and shimmering mirages, the Wild West has forever captured the imagination of adventurers, dreamers, and those daring enough to tread into the unknown. Within this untamed frontier, there lies a mystery as profound as the landscape itself—a region known as the Nevada Triangle, an enigmatic realm teeming with inexplicable phenomena, ghostly apparitions, and chilling tales that reach back to the very roots of the Wild West era.

The Triangle's boundaries are drawn across the harsh desert, its three points encompassing a vast and remote terrain filled with abandoned mines, ghost towns, and the place where the Wild West lives on, not just in history books and faded photographs, but in the very essence of a region that refuses to be tamed, forever calling to those who hear its siren song.

The Phantom Stagecoach of Placerville

In the heart of California's Gold Rush country, nestled among the towering pines and rolling hills, lies the historic town of Placerville. A place steeped in the lore and legends of the Wild West, where the echoes of a bygone era linger in the wind, whispering tales of fortune, adventure, and mystery. Among the most enthralling of these tales is the story of Placerville's phantom stagecoach, a spectral conveyance that haunts the moonlit roads, forever locked in an eternal journey that defies time, logic, and the very fabric of reality.

The stagecoach, once the lifeblood of the Wild West, was a symbol of connection, commerce, and exploration. It carried passengers, mail, and dreams across the vast and untamed frontier, linking isolated communities and bridging the gap once took. Witnesses described it as a grand and elegant coach, pulled by spectral horses and driven by a shadowy figure, its lanterns casting an otherworldly glow. The sight was mesmerising, eerie, and inexplicable, a vision that seemed to transcend the boundaries of the earthly realm.

The accounts were many, and the descriptions eerily consistent. Farmers, travellers, and townsfolk alike claimed to have seen the phantom coach, its appearance always heralded by the distant rumble of hooves and the haunting jingle of harness bells. Some even reported hearing ghostly laughter and the faint strains of music, as if the coach were carrying a lively and invisible party.

Local newspapers began to take interest, and the story spread, capturing the imagination of people far and wide. Sceptics dismissed the sightings as mere hallucinations or hoaxes, but those who had seen the phantom coach could not be swayed. Their experiences were real, tangible, and deeply unsettling.

Theories abound as to the nature of the phantom stagecoach and its eternal journey. Some see in it a symbolic representation of the Wild West itself, a timeless and romantic vision of adventure, risk, and reward. Others believe it to be a manifestation of collective memory, a psychic imprint of a tragic event that left an indelible mark on the land and the people of Placerville.

Among the more supernatural explanations, the notion that the phantom stagecoach is the restless spirit of the Golden Arrow holds a particular fascination. The unresolved mystery, the untold stories of its passengers, and the lost gold all contribute to a narrative that transcends the ordinary, reaching into the realm of myth and magic.

The phantom stagecoach of Placerville continues to capture the imagination, its tale passed down through generations, enriched by each telling, and immortalised in songs, poems, and local folklore. It is a story that resonates with the universal themes of longing, loss, and the human need to connect with the mysterious and the unknown.

In a world that has moved beyond the horse-drawn carriage and the rugged charm of the Wild West, the phantom stagecoach stands as a poignant reminder of a time when roamed the desert landscape, always in search of the elusive glint of gold. He was known to be secretive, guarded, and possessed of a knowledge that set him apart from his fellow miners.

Waltz's story took a dramatic turn when, according to legend, he stumbled upon a hidden cache of gold in the Superstition Mountains, a treasure so vast and pure that it was said to be the richest gold mine in the world. The discovery was monumental, but Waltz never revealed the location of the mine, guarding its secret with a tenacity that bordered on obsession.

Word of the Dutchman's find spread like wildfire, igniting a gold rush that drew men from all walks of life. They came on foot, on horseback, and by wagon, their eyes filled with greed, their hearts pounding with anticipation. They scoured the mountains, dug into the earth, and risked life and limb, all in pursuit of a dream that seemed always just out of reach.

But the Superstition Mountains were not kind to those who sought to plunder their treasures. The terrain was treacherous, the weather unpredictable, and the desert unforgiving. Many who ventured into the mountains never returned, their fate a mystery, their disappearance a chilling testament to the perilous nature of the quest.

As the years passed, the legend of the Lost Dutchman's Gold Mine grew, fed by rumours, half-truths, and wild speculation. The mine became a symbol of human ambition, a tantalising mirage that beckoned with the promise of wealth and adventure but delivered only hardship, despair, and death.

The curse of the mine became an integral part of the legend, a dark and ominous force that seemed to hover over the Superstition Mountains, preying on the greed and folly of those who dared to tread its haunted paths. Mysterious deaths, unexplained phenomena, and tales of ghostly apparitions became synonymous with the mine, adding to its allure and mystique.

Historical accounts abound of those who fell victim to the curse, their stories woven into the fabric of the legend, their experiences a cautionary tale of hubris, obsession, and the inexorable pull of the unknown.

Among the most famous of these accounts is the story of Adolph Ruth, an amateur treasure hunter who ventured into the Superstition Mountains in 1931, armed with maps, clues, and an unshakable belief that he was destined to find the mine. Ruth's expedition ended in tragedy when he vanished without a trace, his skeletal remains found months later, riddled with bullet holes and bearing a cryptic note that only deepened the mystery.

Then there was the tale of Tom Kollenborn, a seasoned prospector and a respected authority on the Lost Dutchman's Gold Mine. Kollenborn spent decades searching for the mine, his quest a lifelong obsession that led him deep into the heart of the Superstition Mountains, where he claimed to have encountered inexplicable phenomena and eerie visions that defied rational explanation.

The list of those who have succumbed to the curse is long, their stories diverse and fascinating, each one a unique and haunting chapter in the saga of the Lost Dutchman's Gold Mine.

The legend lives on, its allure undiminished, its mystery as potent and captivating as ever. The mine remains hidden, its treasures untouched, its location a tantalising enigma that continues to draw treasure hunters from around the world.

In the shadow of the Superstition Mountains, where the sun blazes hot and the nights are filled with the ghostly whisper of the desert wind, the Lost Dutchman's Gold Mine waits, its secrets guarded by a curse that defies time, logic, and human understanding.

It is a place of wonder, terror, and eternal fascination, a place where dreams are forged, and nightmares come to life. It is a place that has become synonymous with the very essence of the Wild West, a place where the line between myth and reality blurs, and where the pursuit of gold becomes a journey into the heart of darkness, obsession, and the unknown.

The Superstition Mountains stand tall and silent, their peaks reaching for the sky, their valleys hiding secrets that may never be revealed. The cursed mine of Superstition

The Fairweather Hotel was once the crown jewel of the bustling mining town. Built in the late 19th century during the height of the Gold Rush, the hotel was a symbol of opulence, a beacon for travellers, miners, and fortune seekers who flocked to the town in search of riches and adventure. Its grand ballroom, luxurious rooms, and exquisite dining facilities made it a hub of social activity, a place where hopes were born, and destinies forged.

But behind the glamour and glitz of the Fairweather Hotel lay a darker truth, a truth that would unravel in the most tragic and unsettling of ways.

The decline began with the exhaustion of the gold veins, and as the town's fortune dwindled, so too did the allure of the Fairweather Hotel. The once-thriving establishment fell into disrepair, its grandeur a fading memory, its halls empty and silent.

It was during this period of decline that the first whispers of something unnatural began to surface. Guests reported strange noises, cold drafts, and eerie sensations. Shadows danced in the corners of rooms, and the faint scent of perfume wafted through corridors that had long lost the warmth of human presence.

The rumours grew, fed by tales of ghostly apparitions, unexplained phenomena, and the chilling account of a young woman who died in one of the hotel's rooms under mysterious circumstances. Her name was Eleanor, and her story would become the tragic centrepiece of the Fairweather Hotel's haunting legacy.

Eleanor was a beautiful and vivacious young woman who came to the town with dreams of love and a new beginning. Her life was cut tragically short, and the circumstances of her death remain shrouded in mystery, rumour, and speculation.

What is known is that her spirit, restless and unfulfilled, lingers in the Fairweather Hotel, her presence a palpable force that has been felt, seen, and documented by those who have dared to venture within the hotel's haunted walls.

Paranormal investigators, historians, and thrill-seekers have delved into the mystery of the Fairweather Hotel, their explorations yielding evidence, anecdotes, and chilling encounters that lend credence to the legend.

Photographs have captured inexplicable anomalies, recordings have picked up ghostly voices, and eyewitness accounts have painted a vivid picture of a haunting that defies logical explanation.

Among the most compelling of these accounts is the story of a paranormal investigator who spent a night in Eleanor's room, only to experience a series of unexplained events that culminated in a terrifying vision of the young woman's ghost, her eyes filled with sorrow, her face etched with the pain of a life cut short.

The haunting of the Fairweather Hotel has become a living testament to the enduring power of the unknown, a chilling reminder of the thin veil that separates the world of the living from the realm of the dead.

The hotel stands, its doors closed, its rooms empty, its halls echoing with the whispers of a past that refuses to be silenced. It is a place where time stands still, where memories linger, and where the tragic story of a young woman's life and death continues to unfold, playing out in the shadows, the echoes, and the ghostly manifestations that have become the Fairweather Hotel's haunting legacy.

It is a story that transcends the ordinary, a tale that resonates with the universal themes of love, loss, and the eternal mystery of what lies beyond the grave.

The Fairweather Hotel is a place where the past lives on, where the echoes of laughter, music, and celebration mingle with the haunting cries of sorrow, despair, and longing.
It is a place that invites exploration, curiosity, and reflection, a place that challenges our understanding of reality and beckons us to peer into the unknown, to listen to the whispers of the past, and to confront the timeless questions that haunt the human soul.

The haunting of the Fairweather Hotel is a story that continues to be told, a legend that grows with each passing year, and a mystery that remains unsolved, forever etched in the annals of folklore, history, and the endless fascination with the paranormal.

Here, in the shadow of the mountains, where the wind howls through the canyons and the night sky is filled with the ghostly glow of a moonlit landscape, the Fairweather Hotel stands as a monument to human dreams, a symbol of a bygone era, and a haunting reminder of the fragile boundary between life and death, reality and myth, and the eternal dance of the seen and the unseen.

It is a place that beckons, that calls out to those who seek to unravel its secrets, and that continues to haunt the imagination, a place where the story of a haunting lives on, a story that is as timeless as the hills, as eternal as the night, and as profound as the mysteries that dwell in the hidden recesses of the human heart.

The Spirits of Cimarron: The St. James Hotel

In the heart of Cimarron, New Mexico, where the trails of the Wild West once crisscrossed and the echoes of gunshots, laughter, and the clinking of poker chips still linger in the air, stands a place of legend, mystery, and ghostly intrigue. It is the St. James Hotel, a timeless edifice that bears the scars of history, the memories of a bygone era, and the haunting presence of spirits that refuse to rest.

The St. James Hotel was more than just a hotel in the heyday of the Wild West; it was a hub, a meeting place, a sanctuary for cowboys, gamblers, lawmen, and infamous figures like Jesse James, Buffalo Bill, and Wyatt Earp. It was a place where destinies were forged, lives were lost, and legends were born.

But the St. James Hotel is more than a relic of history; it is a place where the past lives on, not just in the creaking floorboards, the vintage furnishings, and the bullet holes that punctuate the ceiling of the main saloon but in the spectral manifestations, the ghostly encounters, and the inexplicable phenomena that have made it one of the most haunted places in the Wild West.

The hotel's history is steeped in violence, tragedy, and intrigue. Gunfights were a common occurrence, and the walls bear witness to the lawlessness and wild passions that once ruled the land. Twenty-six men are said to have lost their lives within the hotel's confines, and their restless spirits continue to wander, etching their presence into the fabric of the St. James Hotel's haunting legacy.

Among the most chilling and oft-repeated stories is that of Room 18, a room shrouded in mystery, fear, and the overwhelming sense of something unnatural. It is said to harbour the spirit of an especially restless soul, a presence so potent and unsettling that the room has been locked for years, its secrets hidden, its mystery preserved.

Guests who have stayed near Room 18 have reported strange noises, ghostly apparitions, and a feeling of dread that chills the soul. Some have heard the sound of ghostly footsteps, others have seen shadows that move of their own accord, and still others have felt a spectral hand upon their shoulder, only to turn and find themselves alone.

The haunting of Room 18 is but one chapter in the St. James Hotel's spectral chronicle. There are stories of ghostly gamblers, still engaged in an eternal poker game, their spectral laughter ringing through the halls. There are tales of ghostly cowboys, wandering the corridors, their spurs jingling, their presence a lingering reminder of a time when the West was wild, untamed, and filled with the promise of adventure and the peril of the unknown.

The St. James Hotel is more than a place; it is a living, breathing entity, a vessel that holds the memories, the legends, and the spirits of a time long past but not forgotten.

Paranormal investigators have ventured into the St. James Hotel's haunted rooms and corridors, armed with equipment, curiosity, and the desire to pierce the veil that separates the living from the dead. Their findings have been both intriguing and unsettling, with recorded voices, inexplicable temperature fluctuations, and visual anomalies that defy logical explanation.

Guests, too, have experienced the unexplained, their encounters ranging from the subtle to the profound, from the mysterious to the terrifying. Some have seen spectral figures, others have heard ghostly voices, and still others have felt the icy touch of an unseen hand.

The St. James Hotel's haunting is a complex and multifaceted phenomenon, a tapestry woven from the threads of history, folklore, personal experience, and the intangible essence that dwells in the space between the known and the unknown.

It is a haunting that invites exploration, that challenges our understanding of reality, and that beckons us to step into a world where the boundaries of time, space, and consciousness are fluid, where the past is present, and where the living and the dead coexist in a dance that transcends the ordinary and touches the realm of the extraordinary.

The St. James Hotel is a place where the Wild West lives on, not just in the artefacts, the architecture, and the echoes of a time long past, but in the living presence of the spirits that continue to roam, to haunt, and to tell their stories in ways that defy logic, challenge belief, and inspire wonder.

It is a place where history is more than a collection of facts and events; it is a living, breathing entity that resonates with the energy, the passion, and the indomitable spirit of the Wild West.

Here, in the shadow of the mountains, where the wind whispers through the canyons and the night is filled with the mystery of the unseen, the St. James Hotel stands as a monument to human courage, a testament to human folly, and a haunting reminder of the transient nature of life, the eternal resonance of death, and the profound mystery of what lies beyond the veil of our earthly existence.

The St. James Hotel is a place where legends are born,

where mysteries are preserved, and where the haunting spirits of Cimarron continue to wander, forever etched in the annals of folklore, history, and the human quest to understand the unexplainable.

It is a place that calls to the adventurous, the curious, and the seekers of truth, a place that continues to resonate with the sounds, the sights, and the spectral manifestations of a time that refuses to be silenced, a time that lives on in the memories, the stories, and the haunting presence of the Spirits of Cimarron: The St. James Hotel.

Witches of the West: The Legend of Julia Bulette

In the rugged hills of Virginia City, Nevada, where the echo of pickaxes striking ore still resonates through the tunnels of memory, and where fortune and folly once danced a perilous waltz, there exists a tale as mysterious as the windswept canyons and as enchanting as the desert night. It's the legend of Julia Bulette, a figure who embodied the contradictions of the Wild West, the complexities of human nature, and the mysterious undercurrents of superstition, witchcraft, and the supernatural.

Julia Bulette was a beloved figure in Virginia City, a place known for its silver rush, its colourful characters, and its untamed spirit. She was known for her beauty, her charm, and her generosity. But beneath the facade of respectability and grace, there lay a world of mystery, a realm of practice, and a life that defied convention.

Rumoured to be a witch, Julia's existence was shrouded in enigma, her practices imbued with a mystique that both fascinated and terrified. Was she a sorceress who held sway over the forces of nature? Was she a healer who used her knowledge of herbs, potions, and ancient rituals to cure ailments and ease suffering? Or was she a mere mortal caught in the web of myth, legend, and the human need to believe in the extraordinary?

Julia's life was as rich and textured as the tapestry of the Wild West itself. She was known for her kindness to miners, her philanthropy, and her contributions to the community. Yet, she was also known for her unconventional lifestyle, her alleged connection to the world of the occult, and her rumoured ability to foretell the future, heal the sick, and commune with the unseen forces of the universe.

Her death, too, was shrouded in mystery, a brutal end that left more questions than answers. Was it the work of an envious rival, a scorned lover, or something more sinister, a dark force that reached from the shadows to claim one of its own? The murder of Julia Bulette sent shockwaves through Virginia City, a crime that challenged the values, the beliefs, and the very fabric of a community caught between progress and tradition, reason, and superstition.

The supernatural occurrences that followed her death were no less perplexing. There were those who claimed to have seen her ghost, a spectral figure that roamed the streets of Virginia City, her presence a haunting reminder of a life cut short and a mystery unsolved. There were reports of unexplained phenomena, strange noises, flickering lights, and a pervasive sense of something otherworldly, something that transcended the bounds of earthly existence.

The legend of Julia Bulette is more than a tale of witchcraft and murder; it's a reflection of the Wild West itself, a place where the boundaries between the real and the unreal were porous, where superstition held sway, and where the forces of the unknown were as real as the mountains, the deserts, and the sprawling landscapes that defined a time and a place.

It's a legend that sheds light on the human condition, the human psyche, and the human need to believe in something greater, something mysterious, and something beyond the reach of reason and logic. It's a legend that speaks to the fear of the unknown, the allure of the forbidden, and the eternal dance between light and darkness, good and evil, life and death.

The story of Julia Bulette is a window into a world that defies categorization, a world where witches were both feared and revered, where the lines between science and magic were blurred, and where the mysteries of existence were explored with a mixture of curiosity, awe, and trepidation.

It's a story that resonates with the timeless themes of love, loss, power, and redemption, a story that transcends the confines of history and reaches into the depths of the human soul. It's a story that invites us to question, to ponder, and to reflect on the nature of reality, the power of belief, and the eternal quest for understanding, wisdom, and truth.

The legend of Julia Bulette is a haunting reminder that the Wild West was more than a place of gunslingers, gold rushes, and frontier justice; it was a place of wonder, a place of mysticism, and a place where the forces of the seen and the unseen converged in a dance that continues to fascinate, to intrigue, and to inspire.

In the winds that sweep across the desolate plains, in the shadows that linger in the corners of the mind, and in the whispers that reach from the depths of the past, the legend of Julia Bulette lives on, a spectral presence that haunts the landscape of the imagination, a mysterious force that challenges our perceptions, and a spiritual essence that connects us to the primal, the profound, and the eternal mysteries of existence.

In the land of sagebrush, silver, and endless skies, the story of Julia Bulette is etched in the annals of folklore, history, and the human heart, a story that continues to resonate, to captivate, and to remind us that the Wild West was a place where anything was possible, where reality was malleable, and where the world of the supernatural was as real, as tangible, and as enigmatic as the world of flesh and blood.

It's a story that invites us to step into the realm of the unknown, to explore the boundaries of belief, and to embrace the magic, the mystery, and the eternal allure of the "Witches of the West: The Legend of Julia Bulette."

The Vanishing Town of Ashley, Kansas

In the vast, unyielding expanse of the American West, where the prairie winds whisper tales of dreams and despair, there lies a ghostly scar on the landscape, a void where once stood a community, a heartbeat, a testament to the pioneering spirit. This is the story of Ashley, Kansas, a town that vanished without a trace in 1897, a mystery that transcends time, defies explanation, and continues to echo through the canyons of the human psyche.

Ashley, Kansas was a bustling community, a place where farmers tilled the land, families built their futures, and hope glowed like a lantern in the darkest night. Yet, in the blink of an eye, it vanished, swallowed by an enigma that has puzzled historians, scientists, and seekers of the unknown for more than a century.

The disappearance of Ashley, Kansas, was more than a physical event; it was a metaphysical occurrence, a rupture in the fabric of reality that challenged the very foundations of our understanding of the world. Was it a natural disaster, a freak occurrence of geology or meteorology? Was it a human act, a deliberate erasure by forces unknown and motives unclear? Or was it something else, something that lies beyond the boundaries of reason, science, and human comprehension?

Newspaper reports from the time paint a picture of confusion, terror, and incredulity. There were accounts of strange phenomena, bizarre lights, unexplained noises, and a growing sense of dread that permeated the air, a foreboding that hinted at something otherworldly, something that defied logic, explanation, and the very laws of nature.

Historical records are equally baffling, a patchwork of clues, theories, and dead ends that lead us down a path of intrigue, speculation, and wonder. Was Ashley, Kansas, a victim of an earthquake, a sinkhole, or some other geological event that could explain its sudden and complete disappearance? Was it the work of humans, a conspiracy, a cover-up, or a malicious act of destruction? Or was it something more, something that reaches into the realm of the supernatural, the paranormal, and the unexplained?

The vanishing of Ashley, Kansas, is more than a historical curiosity; it's a philosophical conundrum, a spiritual enigma, and a psychological riddle. It challenges our beliefs, our assumptions, and our very sense of reality. It invites us to question, to probe, and to reflect on the nature of existence, the fragility of our world, and the mysteries that lie just beyond the horizon of our understanding.

It's a story that resonates with the timeless themes of human experience, a story that speaks to our deepest fears, our greatest hopes, and our insatiable curiosity. It's a story that reflects the complexity, the ambiguity, and the paradox of the human condition.

In the world of paranormal folklore, Ashley, Kansas, occupies a special place, a spectral presence that haunts the landscape of the imagination, a ghostly memory that lingers in the shadows of our collective consciousness. It's a story that has inspired books, movies, and countless discussions, a story that continues to fascinate, to intrigue, and to mystify.

Is Ashley, Kansas, a cautionary tale, a warning about the limits of human knowledge and the dangers of human arrogance? Is it a spiritual metaphor, a reflection of the impermanence of life, the transience of existence, and the eternal dance between creation and destruction? Or is it a cosmic riddle, a question without an answer, a mystery without a solution?

In the windswept plains of Kansas, where the echoes of the past reach into the depths of the present, the vanishing town of Ashley is a haunting reminder that our world is a place of wonder, a place of mystery, and a place where the boundaries between the known and the unknown are porous, fluid, and forever shifting.

The story of Ashley, Kansas, is a story that invites us to explore, to ponder, and to embrace the mysteries of existence, the enigmas of life, and the eternal quest for understanding, wisdom, and truth. It's a story that challenges us to reflect on the nature of reality, the power of belief, and the eternal dance between certainty and doubt.

Here, in the heartland of America, where the wild west still lingers in the soul of a nation, the vanishing town of Ashley, Kansas, is etched in the annals of folklore, history, and the human heart, a story that continues to resonate, to captivate, and to remind us that the world is a place of magic, of mystery, and of eternal allure.

It's a story that reaches beyond the confines of time and space, a story that connects us to the primal, the profound, and the eternal mysteries of existence. It's the story of "The Vanishing Town of Ashley, Kansas," a spectral presence that haunts the landscape of the imagination, a mysterious force that challenges our perceptions, and a spiritual essence that invites us to step into the realm of the unknown, to question, to seek, and to embrace the magic, the mystery, and the eternal dance of life.

Ghost Lights of Marfa, Texas: A Luminary Enigma

In the rugged and untamed wilds of Texas, where the echoes of gunshots and the cries of coyotes once filled the air, lies a mystery that has haunted the land since the days of the Wild West. Far from the bustling cities and the clatter of civilization, the desolate plains of Marfa are home to a phenomenon that defies explanation, challenges logic, and beckons the curious and the brave: the ghost lights of Marfa, Texas.

During the late 19th century, when the frontier was still a place of lawlessness and adventure, the first recorded sightings of these mysterious lights began to emerge. Cowboys riding the range under the moonlit sky would see ethereal orbs of light dancing in the distance, following them as they journeyed through the desert. These spectral illuminations, appearing out of nowhere and disappearing just as suddenly, became the subject of hushed conversations around campfires and in the dimly lit saloons of nearby towns.

The lights were described as otherworldly and haunting, glowing with an inner fire that seemed to have a life of its own. They were not merely reflections or mirages but seemed to move with intention, tracking those who observed them, leading them astray, or guiding them to unknown destinations. Many who encountered the lights were filled with a sense of dread, a chilling realisation that they were witnessing something beyond their understanding, something that connected them to the dark and unknown recesses of the universe.

Stories spread like wildfire, turning the ghost lights of Marfa into a legend that resonated with the mystery and danger of the Wild West. Tales were told of prospectors lured to their doom by the lights, mistaking them for the lanterns of fellow miners, only to find themselves lost and alone in the wilderness. Others spoke of ghostly figures, apparitions of long-dead cowboys, or Native American spirits guiding the lights, weaving them into the rich tapestry of folklore and superstition that permeated the frontier.

Attempts to explain the phenomenon were futile. Even as the 20th century dawned and scientific inquiry began to penetrate the myths and legends of the West, the Marfa lights remained an enigma. Researchers and curious travellers alike were drawn to the remote region, hoping to unravel the mystery, but were left confused and awestruck by the lights' elusive nature.

Some hypothesised that the lights were the result of natural gases or atmospheric conditions, but these theories fell short of explaining the lights' sentient behaviour and consistent appearance. Others believed that the lights were the restless souls of the dead, trapped between worlds and seeking redemption or revenge. But the truth remained hidden, obscured by the shadows of uncertainty and the mists of time.

Today, the ghost lights of Marfa continue to intrigue and mystify. The desert plains are no longer filled with the sounds of the Wild West, but the legacy of those bygone days lingers, embodied in the haunting dance of the Marfa lights. Visitors still flock to the area, hoping to catch a glimpse of the lights and to experience the chill of the unknown.

The lights have become a symbol of the unexplainable, a manifestation of the mysteries that lie just beyond our grasp. They are a reminder of a time when the world was filled with wonder and terror, a time when the boundaries between the known and the unknown were blurred, and the veil between the living and the dead was thin.

The ghost lights of Marfa, Texas, are a luminary enigma that transcends the ages, connecting us to the wild and untamed spirit of the frontier. They are a beacon in the darkness, a glimpse into the abyss, and a testament to the enduring power of mystery, fear, and fascination. In the land where the echoes of the past still linger, the lights continue to dance, a haunting and ethereal reminder of the unknown's allure and the human spirit's unquenchable thirst for the strange, the unexplained, and the extraordinary.

The Apparition of Black Jack Ketchum

The legend of Black Jack Ketchum is a tale that echoes through time, a shadowy myth that has become an inseparable part of the fabric of the Wild West. Thomas Edward "Black Jack" Ketchum, an infamous train robber whose audacity and cunning made him a feared and legendary figure, lived a life that was a volatile mix of adventure, crime, and tragedy. But it's in death that his story took on an even darker and more mysterious dimension. His ghost, they say, still haunts the lonely stretches of railway where he once committed his crimes, a spectral figure that continues to instil awe and fear.

Born in San Saba County, Texas, in 1863, Black Jack's early life gave little indication of the path he would eventually follow. The son of a farmer, he grew up in a time when the

West was undergoing profound changes, a time of opportunity and danger, a time when the line between right and wrong was often blurred. It was a time that shaped men like Black Jack, men who chose to live by their own rules, to take what they wanted, and to answer to no one.

As a young man, Black Jack drifted from job to job, never quite finding his place in the world. The West was a land of endless horizons, a place where a man could lose himself or find himself, a place where fate could turn on the roll of a dice or the draw of a gun. It was in this wild and untamed land that Black Jack found his calling. The thrill of the heist, the danger, the cat-and-mouse game with the law; it was a life that suited him, a life that he embraced with a passion that bordered on obsession.

With his brother Sam and a gang of like-minded outlaws, Black Jack embarked on a crime spree that would make him one of the most wanted men in the West. From Texas to New Mexico, they robbed trains, terrorising passengers, and leaving a trail of destruction in their wake. Black Jack's name became synonymous with fear, and his reputation grew with each successful heist.

But with notoriety came attention, and with attention came the relentless pursuit of the law. Black Jack's luck began to run out, and his gang was slowly but surely hunted down. Capture, prison, escape; the cycle repeated itself, a deadly game that could have only one ending. In 1901, Black Jack was captured for the last time, tried, and sentenced to death. His execution was a gruesome affair, a botched hanging that resulted in his decapitation. It was a violent end to a violent life, a fitting epitaph for a man who had lived by the sword.

But death, it seems, was not the end for Black Jack Ketchum. Almost immediately, reports began to emerge of sightings of his ghost. Trainmen, passengers, locals; people from all walks of life claimed to have seen a spectral figure riding alongside the trains, a shadowy apparition that seemed to be in pursuit of something only it could see.

These were not mere figments of the imagination, not simple tales spun around campfires. The reports were detailed, consistent, and compelling. The figure was always described in the same way: a man on horseback, his face obscured by a hat, his eyes glowing with an unnatural light.

The locations were always linked to Black Jack's crimes, the scenes of his triumphs and failures, the places where he had left his mark.

As the years passed, the sightings continued, each one adding to the legend, each one a piece of a puzzle that refused to be solved. Researchers, historians, and paranormal investigators were drawn to the story, each seeking to unravel the mystery, to understand what drove Black Jack's spirit to wander the land he had once roamed in flesh and blood.

Some believe that his ghost is a manifestation of his guilt, a soul tormented by the crimes he committed, unable to find peace. Others see it as a symbol of his defiance, a spirit that refuses to be tamed, that continues to live by its own rules, even in death.

The theories are many, and the answers are few. Scientific investigations have attempted to debunk the sightings, to explain them away as optical illusions or misinterpretations of natural phenomena. But the explanations fall short, unable to account for the sheer number of reports, the consistency of the descriptions, and the unshakeable belief of those who have seen the ghost of Black Jack Ketchum with their own eyes.

The story of Black Jack's ghost is a reflection of the Wild West itself. It's a tale of adventure and danger, of freedom and lawlessness, of dreams and nightmares. It's a story that captures the essence of a time when anything was possible, when heroes and villains were often one and the same, when the landscape was as wild and untamed as the people who lived and died there.

In the end, the legend of Black Jack Ketchum remains an enigma, a story without an ending, a mystery without a solution. His ghost continues to ride the rails, a phantom outlaw whose tale is as timeless as the wind that sweeps across the plains, as eternal as the mountains that stand silent witness to the passing of time. His is a haunting that transcends mere folklore, a haunting that speaks to something deep within us, something that resonates with our own fears and desires, something that reminds us that the past is never truly gone, that the shadows of yesterday continue to reach out and touch us, even in the bright light of today.

The apparition of Black Jack Ketchum is a reminder that the Wild West is still alive, still a part of us, still a place where dreams and ghosts walk hand in hand, where the line between reality and legend is as thin and shifting as the desert sands, where the echoes of a time long gone continue to whisper to us, calling us back to a world where the impossible was possible, where the unbelievable was believed, and where the dead could still reach out and touch the living. It's a haunting that will endure, a legend that will live on, a ghostly presence that will continue to ride the night, a spectral figure that will forever be a part of the wild and untamed land that gave birth to it.

Skinwalkers of the Southwest: Navajo Legends

In the heart of the American Southwest, where the vast desert meets the sky, lies a mystery as profound and ancient as the earth itself. A legend that winds its way through the culture and history of the Navajo people, a tale that resonates with primal fears and unanswered questions. This is the legend of the Skinwalkers, shape-shifting beings that occupy a liminal space between reality and myth, a force that challenges our understanding of nature, culture, and ourselves.

The term "Skinwalker" derives from the Navajo word "yee naaldlooshii," which translates to "with it, he goes on all fours." These are not mere creatures of superstition, but rather beings deeply ingrained in the spiritual and social fabric of the Navajo people. Their stories have been told and retold, passed down from generation to generation, shaping and reflecting the values, beliefs, and fears of a people who have long lived in harmony with the land.

According to the lore, Skinwalkers are witches or practitioners of dark magic who have gained the power to transform themselves into animals. This transformation is not just physical but spiritual, a crossing of boundaries that transcends the limitations of the human form. They are said to move with supernatural speed, to possess the ability to control minds, to curse, to heal, and to destroy.

The stories of encounters with Skinwalkers are both fascinating and terrifying, filled with eerie details and inexplicable events. There are accounts of people being followed by creatures that seemed to be neither human nor animal, of strange noises that chilled the blood, of shadows that moved in ways that defied explanation. Those who have claimed to witness a Skinwalker often describe a feeling of profound unease, a sense that they have stumbled upon something that should not be, something that challenges the very nature of their understanding of the world.

But the legend of the Skinwalkers is not merely a collection of stories or a curiosity of folklore. It is a reflection of a worldview, a way of understanding the world that is holistic, interconnected, and deeply spiritual. It is a belief system that acknowledges the complexity of existence, that recognizes the thin line that separates the human from the non-human, the sacred from the profane.

The Navajo's relationship with the Skinwalkers is nuanced and multifaceted. On one level, they are seen as malevolent, figures to be feared and avoided. But on another level, they represent a kind of wisdom, a recognition of the dual nature of existence, of the delicate balance between light and darkness, good and evil. They are a reminder that the world is not simple or easily understood, that it is a place of mystery, magic, and ambiguity.

Investigating the legend of the Skinwalkers requires a sensitivity to the cultural context in which these stories exist. It is not merely a matter of collecting tales or analysing motifs. It is a process of understanding a way of life, of respecting a tradition that is both ancient and living. It is a journey into a world where myth and reality intertwine, where the spiritual and the material coexist.

The challenge of unravelling the legend of the Skinwalkers is further compounded by the reluctance of the Navajo to speak openly about them. They are considered a taboo subject, something not to be discussed lightly or without proper understanding. This reticence adds to the mystery and the allure, making the Skinwalkers even more enigmatic, even more compelling.

Modern-day interest in the Skinwalkers has grown, with books, documentaries, and even Hollywood movies exploring the legend. This has led to a complex interplay between cultural preservation and commercial exploitation, between respect for tradition and the demands of entertainment. The legend of the Skinwalkers is no longer confined to the Navajo or the Southwest; it has become a part of the global consciousness, a symbol of the universal fascination with the unknown.

In the end, the legend of the Skinwalkers is a mirror that reflects our deepest fears and our most profound questions. It is a narrative that transcends culture and time, that speaks to something fundamental about the human condition. It is a story that reminds us that the world is full of wonder and terror, that we are surrounded by mysteries that may never be solved, that we are part of a web of life that is both beautiful and terrifying.

The Skinwalkers of the Southwest are not just a tale of shape-shifting beings or supernatural occurrences. They are a testament to the complexity of human existence, a challenge to our assumptions, a beacon that guides us towards a greater understanding of ourselves and the world around us.

Whether real or imagined, whether a product of culture or a figment of the mind, the Skinwalkers continue to haunt us, to intrigue us, to call us to explore the boundaries of our understanding. They are a symbol of the Wild West, a place where the frontier is not just a physical space but a metaphysical one, where the known and the unknown meet and merge, where the possible and the impossible coalesce.

They are the spirits of a land that is both ancient and ever-changing, a land that is a repository of dreams and nightmares, a land that is a canvas upon which we paint our hopes, our fears, and our very selves. They are the Skinwalkers of the Southwest, a legend that will endure, a mystery that will continue to fascinate, a luminary enigma that will forever be a part of the tapestry of human imagination.

The Ghost Train of Bostian Bridge

In the early morning hours of August 27, 1891, a thunderous crash echoed through the still air near Statesville, North Carolina, as a westbound passenger train derailed off Bostian Bridge. The horrifying accident claimed the lives of twenty-three people and left many others injured. The twisted metal and broken bodies were a gruesome testament to the tragic event that would sear itself into local memory. But the story did not end with the recovery and mourning; it gave birth to a legend that persists to this day. A spectral train, replaying its last moments on the anniversary of the disaster, became a haunting legacy of Bostian Bridge.

The events leading up to the crash were as ordinary as any other day. The train, filled with passengers eager to reach their destinations, steamed across the picturesque North Carolina landscape. As it approached Bostian Bridge, something went terribly wrong. Travelling at a high speed, the locomotive leaped from the tracks and plunged into the creek below. The screams of terror and sounds of crushing wood and metal marked the end of what should have been a routine journey.

As with many catastrophic events, the reasons behind the crash were meticulously investigated. Human error, mechanical failure, even sabotage were considered. The subsequent inquiry ruled out foul play, and the final report suggested that the train was simply moving too fast for the curve leading up to the bridge. It was a conclusion that did little to comfort the grieving families, a rational explanation for an event that felt anything but ordinary.

Soon after the tragedy, stories began to emerge of strange occurrences near Bostian Bridge. People who ventured close to the site on the anniversary of the crash claimed to hear the distant whistle of a train, the churning of wheels, and the cries of the passengers. Some even reported seeing a ghostly locomotive, complete with spectral passengers, making its way towards the bridge before vanishing into the night.

These accounts were not the idle talk of impressionable minds. People from different walks of life, with no reason to lie, swore to have witnessed the phantom train. As the years went by, the story of the Ghost Train of Bostian Bridge became a fixture of local folklore, a chilling reminder of the past, and a mystery that drew both believers and sceptics.

Modern-day investigations have attempted to get to the bottom of the phenomenon. Paranormal researchers, armed with sophisticated equipment, have camped near the bridge, hoping to capture evidence of the ghost train. Some have recorded unexplained noises; others have documented fluctuations in temperature and electromagnetic fields. Yet, the ghost train itself has remained elusive, a phenomenon that defies easy explanation.

Historians have delved into the archives, uncovering documents, photographs, and firsthand accounts of the crash. The human stories behind the tragedy have added depth and context to the legend, transforming it from a mere ghost story into a poignant tale of loss, grief, and remembrance. The faces and names of the victims, the circumstances of their lives, and the impact of their deaths on their families and community have made the ghost train a symbol of a time and a place, a connection to a past that continues to resonate.

The Ghost Train of Bostian Bridge is more than a paranormal curiosity. It is a reflection of our collective fascination with the unknown, our need to make sense of the inexplicable, and our desire to connect with history in a tangible way. It is a story that transcends the boundaries of time and place, that speaks to universal themes of tragedy, memory, and mystery.

In the realm of the Wild West, where frontier life was fraught with danger and uncertainty, the ghost train takes its place among the many legends that capture the imagination. It is a tale that reminds us that the past is never truly gone, that the echoes of bygone days can still be heard if we listen closely enough. It is a story that challenges our understanding of reality and invites us to consider the possibility that there are things beyond our comprehension.

Whether a product of mass hysteria, a trick of the mind, or something genuinely supernatural, the Ghost Train of Bostian Bridge remains an enduring enigma. It is a tale that continues to be told, a legend that still draws the curious, the brave, and the sceptical. It is a haunting legacy of a tragic event, a spectral reminder of the thin line that separates the living from the dead, the real from the unreal, the ordinary from the extraordinary.

In the shadow of Bostian Bridge, where the physical evidence of the crash has long since vanished, the ghost train lives on, a phantom echo of a world that once was. It is a testament to the power of story, the resilience of memory, and the enduring fascination with the unexplained. It is the Ghost Train of Bostian Bridge, a luminary enigma in the tapestry of American folklore, a haunting melody in the symphony of our shared history.

Cholera Springs: The Haunted Well

In the parched landscape of the Wild West, where water was more precious than gold, lay a small settlement known as Cholera Springs. The heart of this settlement was a deep, mysterious well that provided life-sustaining water to the residents. But as the decades wore on, the well became synonymous with death and despair. It wasn't just water that echoed from its dark depths; whispers of lost souls and ghostly apparitions became a part of its lore. The Haunted Well of Cholera Springs, as it came to be known, is a tale that weaves tragedy, superstition, and the inexplicable into a tapestry that still chills the bones of those who dare to approach it.

The story begins in the summer of 1867 when a wagon train of hopeful settlers arrived at the spot that would become Cholera Springs. At first, the well was a blessing, offering a seemingly endless supply of fresh water in an otherwise arid land. The settlers established their homes, planted crops, and dared to dream of a prosperous life on the frontier.

But their dreams turned to nightmares when a cholera outbreak swept through the settlement. Cholera, a virulent and often fatal disease, struck without warning, leaving families decimated and the community in fear. Many succumbed to the illness, their bodies hastily buried in shallow graves near the well. The exact source of the contagion was never determined, but whispers began that the well itself was cursed, a harbinger of death rather than life.

The haunting began not long after the outbreak was contained. Residents reported hearing voices near the well, faint cries of distress, and sometimes laughter, an eerie sound that chilled the blood. Some even claimed to have seen ghostly figures around the well, pale and translucent, forever bound to the place of their suffering.

As years turned into decades, the settlement at Cholera Springs dwindled. The haunting of the well, however, did not abate. Those who dared to approach it continued to report strange occurrences, a sense of dread that clung to the place like a shroud. Tales of the Haunted Well spread beyond the region, drawing the curious, the sceptical, and those with a penchant for the unknown.

Modern-day paranormal investigators have been drawn to Cholera Springs, eager to unravel the truth behind the legends. Armed with sophisticated equipment designed to detect even the faintest trace of supernatural activity, they have ventured to the well, recording their findings and attempting to communicate with whatever might linger there.

The results have been both tantalising and confounding. Some have captured unexplained noises, others have reported sudden drops in temperature, and still others have experienced feelings of unease and terror that defy logical explanation. The well, it seems, continues to guard its secrets, reluctant to reveal the truth behind the haunting.

Historians, too, have explored the story of Cholera Springs, unearthing documents, diaries, and firsthand accounts that shed light on the lives of the settlers, the cholera outbreak, and the aftermath. The human tragedy that unfolded at the well is heart-wrenching, a stark reminder of the fragility of life on the frontier and the thin line between hope and despair.

The Haunted Well of Cholera Springs is not just a ghost story; it is a reflection of a time and a place where life was a constant struggle, where the unknown lurked around every corner, and where superstition and belief in the supernatural were often all that people had to make sense of the world. It is a story that resonates with universal themes of loss, fear, and the eternal quest to understand the inexplicable.

The well itself, now weathered and forlorn, still stands as a silent witness to the history that unfolded at its edge. It is a physical link to a past that continues to echo in the present, a monument to both human endurance and human frailty.

In the lore of the Wild West, where truth often melds with

myth, the Haunted Well of Cholera Springs occupies a unique place. It is a tale that transcends the boundaries of time, that speaks to our deepest fears and our never-ending fascination with the unknown. It is a story that invites us to ponder the mysteries of existence and to consider the possibility that there are realms beyond our understanding, places where the living and the dead intersect, where history lingers, and where the voices of the past continue to whisper their haunting melody.

The well at Cholera Springs, with its dark depths and ghostly echoes, remains a luminary enigma in the annals of American folklore. It is a place where the ordinary becomes the extraordinary, where the rational gives way to the mysterious, and where a simple well becomes a portal to another dimension, a chilling reminder of the complex tapestry of human existence.

The Ghostly Children of San Antonio's Railroad Tracks

In the vast expanse of the American Southwest, where the frontier once teemed with cowboys, settlers, and tales of adventure, a legend has taken root—one that echoes across time and transcends the typical ghost stories of the Wild West. The legend of the Ghostly Children of San Antonio's Railroad Tracks not only resonates with the mystique of bygone days but also tugs at the very fabric of human emotion. It's a story that links the present to the past, where echoes of the Wild West linger and the ethereal touch of ghostly children can still be felt.

The tale begins in the late 19th century, a time when San Antonio, Texas, was a bustling hub for trade and transportation. The railroad was a symbol of progress and opportunity, connecting remote frontier towns with the rest of the nation. But for all its promise, the railroad also bore witness to tragedy.

According to local lore, a school bus filled with children was crossing the railroad tracks on a foggy morning. The driver, perhaps unfamiliar with the area or caught unaware by the thick mist, stalled the bus directly on the tracks. Panic ensued as the distant rumble of an oncoming train grew louder. Despite the frantic screams and desperate attempts to move the bus, it was too late. The train collided with the stalled vehicle, and the lives of all the children on board were lost in an instant.

In the wake of this heart-wrenching tragedy, strange occurrences began to manifest around the site of the accident. Drivers who found themselves in trouble on the tracks would feel their cars being gently pushed to safety by unseen hands. Mysterious handprints, small and delicate, would appear on the back of vehicles, and ethereal laughter could be heard, lingering in the air.

Over time, these accounts grew in number and detail, transforming the railroad tracks into a place of reverence and wonder. It was as if the children who had perished so tragically were still there, still watching over those who ventured near the tracks, still reaching out to help.

But the story of the Ghostly Children of San Antonio's Railroad Tracks is more than a haunting tale. It's a window into the Wild West, a reflection of a time when life was both simpler and more perilous, when the frontier was a place of adventure and uncertainty, and when legends were born from the intersection of fact and folklore.

In the 1800s, San Antonio was a bustling frontier town, alive with the spirit of the West. Cowboys, settlers, prospectors, and adventurers all converged on this vibrant hub, each contributing to the rich tapestry of stories and legends that would become part of the region's cultural heritage.

The railroad played a crucial role in shaping the West, bringing people, goods, and ideas to remote areas, and forging connections between isolated communities. It was a symbol of progress and modernity, but it also brought danger and tragedy. Accidents were not uncommon, and the railroad became a setting for both triumph and loss.

The story of the ghostly children reflects this duality. It's a tale of tragedy and hope, of loss and redemption. It speaks to the enduring human need to make sense of the inexplicable, to find meaning in suffering, and to connect with something greater than ourselves.

As the legend grew, it became a focal point for paranormal enthusiasts and historians alike. Investigations were conducted, some with scientific rigour, others with a more mystical approach. Unexplained phenomena were recorded, from strange lights to electromagnetic anomalies. Sceptics and believers debated the evidence, but the allure of the ghostly children remained undiminished.

The cultural impact of the legend extended beyond the boundaries of San Antonio. It inspired art, literature, music, and film, becoming a symbol of the complex interplay between history, memory, and myth. It resonated with people from all walks of life, transcending geographical and generational divides.

At its core, the legend of the Ghostly Children of San Antonio's Railroad Tracks is a reflection of the Wild West itself—a landscape filled with beauty and danger, a frontier where reality and imagination blend, and a region where the past continues to shape the present.

It's a haunting that invites us to reflect on our own connections to history, to ponder the mysteries of existence, and to embrace the idea that even in death, there can be purpose and connection.

In the grand narrative of the American West, where ghost towns, cursed mines, and spectral cowboys abound, the ghostly children occupy a unique place. They are a reminder that the Wild West is not just a chapter in history but a living, breathing entity that continues to fascinate, inspire, and haunt us.

The railroad tracks of San Antonio, now weathered by time, still bear witness to the legend. They stand as a testament to the enduring power of storytelling, to the human capacity for empathy, and to the timeless allure of the unknown. They invite us to pause, to listen, and to believe in the extraordinary.

As the sun sets over the frontier, casting long shadows and painting the sky with hues of orange and pink, one can almost hear the laughter of the ghostly children, see their small hands reaching out, and feel their presence, as real and tangible as the wind that sweeps across the plains.

In the end, the legend of the Ghostly Children of San Antonio's Railroad Tracks is not just a ghost story. It's a celebration of the Wild West, a tribute to the human spirit, and a reminder that the past is never truly gone. It lingers in the places we least expect, waiting to be rediscovered, waiting to tell its story once again.

Bannack, Montana: A Town Frozen in Time

Nestled in the rolling hills of southwestern Montana, far from the hustle and bustle of modern life, lies Bannack, a ghost town that whispers secrets of the Wild West. Once a thriving mining town, it now stands eerily preserved, a town frozen in time, where the echoes of the past linger and the air is thick with the inexplicable.

Founded in 1862 during the gold rush, Bannack was a beacon for those seeking fortune and opportunity. Miners, merchants, cowboys, and settlers all flocked to this promising frontier outpost. Streets buzzed with activity, saloons brimmed with laughter, and the clatter of horseshoes filled the air. It was a place of dreams and aspirations, where the promise of gold ignited a fire in the hearts of many.

But as the gold dried up, so did the lifeblood of the town. Businesses shuttered, families moved on, and Bannack's once-vibrant pulse began to fade. By the early 20th century, the town was abandoned, left to the mercy of time and the elements.

Today, Bannack stands as a testament to a bygone era. Its wooden buildings, though weathered and worn, retain an uncanny authenticity. Doors creak on rusty hinges, windows peer out like hollow eyes, and the wind whispers through the cracks, as if carrying the voices of those who once called Bannack home.

Visitors to Bannack often speak of a profound sense of history, a palpable connection to the Wild West. But for many, the experience goes beyond mere nostalgia. Tales of paranormal activity abound, lending an air of mystery and intrigue to this already enigmatic place.

The ghost of Dorothy Dunn, a young girl who tragically drowned in a dredge pond, is said to haunt the area around her watery grave. Dressed in a blue dress, her spectral figure has been spotted by numerous witnesses, sometimes appearing to beckon or wave before vanishing into thin air.

In the old Hotel Meade, the cries of a ghostly child have been heard, along with the footsteps of invisible patrons. The spirit of a woman in a long, flowing gown has been seen gliding down the staircase, her face obscured by a haunting veil.

Bannack's courthouse, which also served as a makeshift gallows, is a hotbed of supernatural occurrences. Cold spots, unexplained noises, and ghostly apparitions have all been reported within its darkened chambers. Some even claim to have seen the ghost of the infamous sheriff, Henry Plummer, who was hanged for his alleged crimes.

These tales, chilling as they are, raise important questions about the nature of ghost towns and why they become focal points for paranormal activity. Is it the tragic history, the unfulfilled dreams, or the abrupt abandonment that gives rise to these ghostly manifestations? Or is there something inherent in the fabric of such places, a residual energy that clings to the very walls and streets?

Scholars and paranormal investigators have ventured into Bannack to seek answers. Through a blend of historical research, eyewitness testimonies, and scientific methods, they have sought to unravel the complexities of this haunted landscape.

Some argue that the preservation of Bannack, with its untouched buildings and artefacts, creates a conduit to the past, allowing the energy and emotions of its former inhabitants to resonate. Others point to the collective consciousness, the shared stories, and folklore that breathe life into the legends and make them part of the cultural fabric.

The phenomenon of ghost towns, and Bannack, in particular, reveals much about our relationship with history and memory. They are liminal spaces, where the past and the present converge, where the tangible and the ethereal coexist. They challenge our perceptions of time and reality and invite us to explore the unknown.

In Bannack, the Wild West lives on, not just as a chapter in a history book but as a living, breathing entity. The town's spectral inhabitants, the creaking floorboards, the winds that carry the scent of gunpowder and whiskey—they all contribute to a hauntingly beautiful tapestry that captures the essence of the frontier.

Visiting Bannack is like stepping into a time machine, where the boundaries between then and now blur, and the ghosts of the past reach out to touch the living. It's a place where history is not just remembered but relived, where legends are not just told but experienced.

As the sun dips below the horizon and the shadows lengthen, Bannack takes on a surreal quality. The silence deepens, the temperature drops, and the town's ghostly residents seem to awaken. Whether real or imagined, their presence is felt, their stories resonate, and their legacy endures.

Bannack, Montana, is more than a ghost town. It's a repository of dreams and memories, a place where the Wild West is still alive, still whispering its tales of adventure, tragedy, and mystery. It's a place where the past refuses to die, where the ghosts of a golden era continue to roam, and where the allure of the unknown beckons to those willing to listen.

In the grand tapestry of the American frontier, Bannack occupies a unique place. It's a town frozen in time, a hauntingly beautiful relic that continues to captivate, inspire, and challenge our understanding of history and the supernatural. It's a place where the Wild West still lives, a place where ghosts walk, and a place where legends never die.

The Mystery of Devil's Tower: Sacred and Supernatural

Rising ominously from the flatlands of northeastern Wyoming, Devil's Tower stands as a testament to the earth's mysterious forces and humankind's endless fascination with the unknown. This geological marvel, with its unique hexagonal columns, has long captured the imagination of those who gaze upon it. It is a place of natural wonder, spiritual significance, and supernatural intrigue.

Devil's Tower, or "Bear Lodge" as it is known by Native American tribes, has been a sacred site for thousands of years. Many tribes, including the Lakota, Cheyenne, and Kiowa, have their legends and stories intertwined with the formation of the tower. For them, it is not merely a striking geological feature but a living entity with deep spiritual connections.

One Lakota legend tells of seven young girls being pursued by giant bears. In their desperation, they climbed atop a rock and prayed to the Great Spirit for salvation. Hearing their pleas, the Great Spirit raised the rock, causing the bears to leave deep claw marks as they tried to reach the girls. The marks remain etched in the tower's sides, and the girls were transformed into the Pleiades star cluster.

This legend, like many others, emphasises a profound connection between the physical landscape, the celestial bodies, and the spiritual realm. It reveals a worldview in which everything is interconnected and sacred.

But the mystical aura of Devil's Tower extends beyond Native American lore. In more recent times, it has become associated with UFO sightings and extraterrestrial encounters. Its unusual appearance has led some to speculate that it may be an ancient beacon or landing site for alien spacecraft.

In the 1970s, the area around Devil's Tower witnessed a

surge in UFO sightings, with many observers reporting strange lights, unexplained noises, and even close encounters with otherworldly beings. These reports have contributed to the tower's reputation as a hotspot for paranormal activity and have drawn UFO enthusiasts from around the world.

The 1977 film "Close Encounters of the Third Kind" further cemented Devil's Tower's connection to the extraterrestrial by using it as a central location for human-alien communication. The film's portrayal of the tower as a meeting point between worlds resonated with many and added another layer to its already rich tapestry of mystery and wonder.

But what is it about Devil's Tower that inspires such awe and fascination? Is it merely its striking appearance, or is there something more profound at play?

Many who visit Devil's Tower speak of an intense spiritual energy that permeates the site. Some describe feelings of peace and transcendence, while others report strange vibrations or sensations. Healers and spiritual seekers are often drawn to the tower, believing it to be a vortex or conduit for divine energy.

Scientists, too, are intrigued by the tower's formation, which remains a subject of debate and research. Its hexagonal columns, formed through the cooling and cracking of molten rock, are a geological enigma. While there are theories to explain its creation, the precise process is still not fully understood, adding to the tower's mystique.

The interplay between the sacred, the scientific, and the supernatural at Devil's Tower is a complex and fascinating phenomenon. It reveals the multifaceted ways in which we engage with the unknown and how we seek to make sense of the inexplicable.

Devil's Tower challenges our perceptions of reality, inviting us to explore the boundaries between the earthly and the ethereal, the mundane and the mystical. It is a place where history and legend merge, where science and spirituality coalesce, and where the natural and the supernatural intertwine.

Through the Native American stories, the UFO encounters, and the spiritual experiences, Devil's Tower emerges as a symbol of humanity's eternal quest for understanding and connection. It stands as a beacon, calling us to look beyond the surface, to question our assumptions, and to delve into the mysteries of existence.

In the context of the Wild West, a landscape often associated with rugged individualism and frontier exploration, Devil's Tower takes on added significance. It embodies the spirit of discovery and the courage to venture into the unknown. It is a reminder of our shared heritage, our collective curiosity, and our unquenchable thirst for knowledge.

As the sun sets and the stars begin to twinkle, Devil's Tower casts a long shadow over the land, a silhouette that seems to reach across time and space. It is a sentinel of the past, a harbinger of the future, and a symbol of the eternal now.

In the end, Devil's Tower is more than a geological marvel or a cultural landmark. It is a living testament to the power of the human imagination, the resilience of ancient traditions, and the enduring allure of the mysterious. It is a place where the earthly meets the divine, where the physical touches the metaphysical, and where the boundaries between this world and the next blur into a dance of wonder and possibility. In the vast tapestry of the Wild West, it stands as a singular point of convergence, a nexus where the sacred and the supernatural come alive, forever etched in the hearts and minds of those who dare to explore its depths.

Spectral Cowboys: The Ghosts of Dead Man's Hole

Deep in the heart of Texas lies a place that sends chills down the spine of those who dare to venture near it. Known as Dead Man's Hole, this dark, foreboding well has become synonymous with spectral cowboys and ghostly legends. Its haunting reputation has transcended generations, weaving itself into the very fabric of Wild West folklore.

Dead Man's Hole, located near Marble Falls, is a natural limestone well, some 155 feet deep, with a reputation as a repository for the bodies of the lawless or those unfortunate enough to cross paths with hidden dangers. Its history is steeped in tales of murder, treachery, and the harsh realities of life on the frontier.

But it's not just the grim past that lingers at Dead Man's

Hole; it is said that the ghosts of spectral cowboys roam the area, forever tied to the place of their demise. Witnesses have reported eerie sights and sounds, including phantom hoofbeats, ghostly figures on horseback, and chilling whispers in the wind.

The legends surrounding Dead Man's Hole take root in the turbulent times of the Civil War and Reconstruction. Stories abound of Confederate sympathisers and outlaws meeting their end at the well, either through betrayal or justice meted out by vigilantes. It was said that bodies dropped into the hole would disappear, swallowed by the abyss, leaving behind only echoes and shadows.

One haunting tale tells of a cowboy who was murdered for his land and gold, his body hidden in the well's depths. Since that fateful day, travellers near Dead Man's Hole have reported seeing his ghostly visage, forever riding his spectral horse, searching for justice and perhaps a final resting place.

But why does the image of the spectral cowboy resonate so deeply in our collective imagination? What is it about these ghostly figures that capture the essence of the Wild West?

The cowboy has long been a symbol of the American frontier, embodying values of independence, courage, and rugged individualism. They were explorers and adventurers, taming the wilderness and forging a path through an untamed land. In the spectral cowboys of Dead Man's Hole, these archetypes are both preserved and subverted.

The ghosts of Dead Man's Hole represent a darker side of the cowboy mythos, a reminder of the lawlessness and violence that often lurked beneath the romanticised surface. They are figures trapped in a liminal state, caught between life and death, the physical and the spiritual. Their haunting presence serves as a metaphor for the untamed nature of the frontier, a place where danger was ever-present, and the line between civilization and chaos was razor-thin.

Modern-day explorers of Dead Man's Hole, including paranormal investigators, have sought to uncover the truth behind the legends. Some have come away convinced of the well's supernatural energy, while others remain sceptical. Yet, the allure of the spectral cowboys persists, a ghostly echo of a time long past.

The tales of Dead Man's Hole also reflect a universal fascination with places of mystery and danger. Wells, caves, and other underground spaces often figure in folklore as portals to the underworld or as repositories for hidden truths. In Dead Man's Hole, these elements converge, creating a place where the known and the unknown meet, where the past mingles with the present, and where the living can touch the spectral.

In examining the haunting of Dead Man's Hole, we delve into the heart of the Wild West, uncovering layers of history, myth, and symbolism. We encounter a world where reality blends with fantasy, where the frontier's stark realities give way to the endless possibilities of the imagination.

We are left to ponder the nature of ghosts and why certain places become imbued with supernatural significance. Is it merely the product of human psychology, our need to make sense of the unexplainable, or is there something more profound at work? Do the spectral cowboys of Dead Man's Hole still wander, restless and unbound, a testament to the human spirit's indomitable will?

Dead Man's Hole continues to fascinate and terrify, a place where the legends of the Wild West come to life in the most unexpected ways. It serves as a reminder that our world is full of mysteries, waiting to be explored, and that the ghosts of the past may still walk among us, whispering secrets in the wind, forever etched in the landscape of our dreams and our fears.

The haunting of Dead Man's Hole is more than just a ghost story; it's a glimpse into the soul of the Wild West, a reflection of our deepest hopes and darkest fears, and a symbol of a time when the boundaries between the earthly and the ethereal were as fluid and elusive as the spectral cowboys themselves. It stands as a singular point in the rich tapestry of American folklore, a haunting melody that continues to resonate, long after the last echoes have faded into the night.

The Haunting Melodies of the Ghost Dancer

The sound of ghostly melodies filtering through the cold desert night is a tale that has captivated many travellers and locals in the remote regions of the American West. The story, both fascinating and chilling, centres around an abandoned saloon where, under the pale glow of the moon, ethereal tunes can still be heard playing, as if a spectral musician continues to perform for an audience long gone.

At the heart of this haunting tale is the Ghost Dance movement, a spiritual practice that swept through various Native American tribes in the late 19th century. It was a dance of desperation, of hope, and of a longing for a return to a time before the white settlers came.

The Ghost Dance was more than mere ritual; it was an

embodiment of a profound cultural shift, a symbol of resistance, and a beacon of hope for many Native Americans. The dance's origin can be traced to the teachings of the Paiute prophet Wovoka, who promised that the dance would reunite the living with the spirits of the dead, bring peace, and usher in a new era where Native American lands would be restored.

In the midst of this historical backdrop, the legend of the ghost dancer emerged. The story is often localised, set in an unnamed frontier town, at a time when saloons were the pulsing heart of social life. They were places of joy, sorrow, and sometimes even violence.

The ghost dancer was said to be a musician who once played in a thriving saloon, a place alive with the sound of laughter, clinking glasses, and the rhythmic thud of dancing boots. He was a part of the lifeblood of the Wild West, providing melodies for the living to dance to. Yet, his story was destined to become intertwined with the spiritual movement that was gripping the Native American communities.

A tragedy struck the saloon, details of which vary from one telling to the next. Fire, a deadly brawl, a broken heart—each version of the story adds its own flavour to the legend. What remains consistent, however, is that the musician met an untimely death, and with him, the music died too.

Or so it seemed.

The saloon was eventually abandoned, left to the mercy of the elements and time. But the locals and passing wanderers would whisper about a haunting melody, a tune that would drift through the broken windows and decaying wood of the old building. It was a sound both beautiful and terrifying, a lingering echo of a time long past.

The connection between the ghost dancer and the Ghost Dance movement is not merely in name but in spirit. Just as the Ghost Dance was a call for restoration and a bridge between the living and the dead, the ghostly melodies of the saloon were a bridge to a bygone era, a sonic reminder of a world that once was.

Some believe the haunting melodies are the musician's

eternal tribute to the ideals of the Ghost Dance, a continuous performance that transcends death. Others see it as a symbol of the enduring power of music and culture, even in the face of loss and change.

The cultural significance of the haunting melodies goes beyond mere superstition or folklore. It taps into a collective memory, a shared understanding of displacement, sorrow, and longing. It's a reflection of a time when the West was wild, when life was a delicate dance between joy and despair, and when music could be both an escape from reality and a profound expression of the human soul.

Modern-day explorations of the abandoned saloon have yielded mixed accounts. Some claim to have heard the ghostly tunes; others find only silence. Sceptics may dismiss the legend as mere fancy, but for those who believe, the haunting melodies of the ghost dancer remain a real and potent symbol.

The legend of the ghost dancer, with its rich historical connections and evocative imagery, provides a captivating lens through which to explore the complex tapestry of the Wild West. It's a story that resonates with the power of music, the resilience of culture, and the timeless dance between life and death.

By chronicling this haunting tale, we touch a nerve that runs deep in the American psyche, a yearning for connection to a past that is both beautiful and tragic. The ghostly melodies continue to play, a spectral refrain that echoes through the ages, inviting us to listen, to remember, and to dance once more to the haunting tunes of a world that once was.

The Phantom Prospector of Death Valley

In the desolate stretches of Death Valley, where the sun scorches the earth and the very air seems to waver with heat, there stalks a figure as enigmatic as the shifting sands. A phantom prospector, spectral and gaunt, lantern swinging in a skeletal hand, forever seeking his lost fortune, haunting the very landscape that both seduced and betrayed him. His story is a chilling tale that echoes across time, resonating with the greed, despair, and dark mysteries of the human heart.

The legend of the phantom prospector dates back to the wild days of the Gold Rush when men were driven to madness in their search for wealth. Some say the prospector was once a man who struck gold in the barren valley, only to have it cruelly snatched away. Others tell of a miner who ventured too far into the merciless desert, his mind unhinged by thirst and the tantalising glimmer of unseen riches.

What all the tales agree upon is the haunting presence of the ghostly miner. His appearance is said to be otherworldly, with hollow eyes that gleam like nuggets of gold, and a gaunt face weathered by the desert winds. His clothes hang in tatters, relics of a bygone era, and his voice, when heard, is like the distant howl of the wind.

Travellers and fortune-seekers who have ventured into Death Valley have reported chilling encounters with the phantom prospector. Some speak of ghostly singing heard in the dead of night, a mournful melody that speaks of loss and unending yearning. Others have seen the spectral figure by the light of the moon, his shadowy form gliding over the dunes, lantern swinging, leading them to places where the very earth seems to whisper of hidden gold.

The area known as Furnace Creek, a place teeming with old mining camps and forgotten dreams, has become a focal point for sightings of the phantom prospector. Here, amidst the decaying remnants of a time long past, the ghostly miner is said to make his presence known, especially on windless nights when the desert lays silent and time seems to stand still.

Some accounts are particularly spine-chilling. A group of campers once told of waking to find their equipment scattered and gold dust sprinkled around their campsite, the air heavy with a sense of unseen eyes watching. Another tale speaks of a miner who followed the phantom's lantern deep into a hidden canyon, only to find himself lost, the ghostly light vanishing as suddenly as it appeared, leaving him to wander alone and terrified.

Paranormal investigators have been drawn to Death Valley, lured by the legend and the challenge of unravelling the mystery. EVP recordings have captured unexplained voices, murmuring about gold and betrayal. Photographs have shown ethereal glows and strange shadows that defy logical explanation.

The haunting story of the phantom prospector is more than just a ghost tale; it's a complex tapestry that weaves together the greed that drove men into the inhospitable desert, the cruelty of nature, and the eternal human desire for something just beyond reach. It's a story that reflects the very essence of the Wild West, with its limitless horizons, unfathomable dangers, and the ever-present dance with death.

The spectral miner of Death Valley continues to captivate and terrify, a symbol of both the romance and the ruthlessness of an era that has passed but is not forgotten. In his endless search for gold, in his mournful song that drifts across the desert, he represents the timeless struggle between man and nature, dreams and reality, life and the shadowy realm beyond.

The phantom prospector of Death Valley lingers, a chilling presence that reminds us of the thin veil between this world and the next, of the eternal dance of hope and despair, and of the dark allure of unquenchable desire. He stands as a ghostly sentinel, a keeper of secrets, a whispering wind that carries with it the essence of the Wild West, its triumphs and tragedies, its dreams and its nightmares, forever etched in the golden sands of time.

El Paso's Haunted Hotel: The De Soto

Deep in the heart of El Paso, Texas, stands the De Soto Hotel, an architectural marvel that dates back to the early days of the 20th century. Its regal exterior and sumptuous interiors are a testament to a bygone era, a time when the Wild West was transitioning into modernity, yet the rugged spirit of the frontier still held sway.

Nestled amidst the bustling city streets, the De Soto has long been a symbol of El Paso's growth and prosperity. It was envisioned as a beacon of luxury and sophistication, a place where the rich and the influential would gather, where opulence was the norm, and where every whim was catered to with grace and elegance.

Yet beneath this façade of grandiosity lies a dark and

enigmatic legacy, one that has earned the De Soto the reputation of being one of the most haunted hotels in Texas. The halls, once filled with laughter and music, now echo with whispers of the past, and shadows dance in the corners, as if hinting at something just beyond the realm of the living.

The history of the De Soto is intertwined with the very land upon which it was built. Native American tribes once roamed these grounds, their spirits imbuing the place with a mystical energy. Legends speak of battles and sacred ceremonies, of a connection with the earth that transcended the mundane. It's as if the very soil upon which the hotel stands is alive with memories, and those memories have seeped into the walls, creating a tapestry of emotions and echoes that resonate to this day.

Within the De Soto's ornate rooms and winding corridors reside several spectral inhabitants, each with its unique story and characteristics. The most famous of these is the Lady in Red, a tragic figure who roams the hotel, her spectral form adorned in a flowing red gown. Her story is one of love, loss, and betrayal, and her presence is often accompanied by the soft scent of roses and the faint sound of sobbing.

Then there are the Ghostly Children, their laughter a haunting melody that floats through the air. They have been seen playing in the grand ballroom, their innocent games tinged with an underlying sense of eeriness. Some say they are the spirits of children who once resided in the hotel, their lives tragically cut short.

The Mysterious Bellman, too, makes his presence known, assisting guests in an old-fashioned uniform, his face an emotionless mask. His actions are courteous, yet his very being sends a chill down the spine, as if he's a messenger from another realm.

The stories of hauntings at the De Soto are not confined to legend. Guests and staff alike have experienced the unexplainable. There are tales of phantom footsteps, of doors opening and closing on their own, of voices whispering in empty rooms. Photographs have captured inexplicable shadows, and recordings have picked up voices from the beyond.

Modern-day paranormal investigators have sought to unravel the mysteries of the De Soto, employing technology and scientific methods. They have documented temperature drops, electromagnetic field fluctuations, and other phenomena that defy logical explanation. Yet, despite all efforts, the De Soto remains an enigma, its secrets locked away, waiting for the right moment to be revealed.

The allure of the De Soto has transcended its physical boundaries, turning it into a cultural icon. It has become a place of pilgrimage for those drawn to the unknown, for those seeking a connection with something greater than themselves. Ghost tours are conducted, books are written, and documentaries are filmed, all in an attempt to capture the essence of the De Soto's haunting beauty.

But beyond the ghostly manifestations and the thrill of the unknown, the De Soto stands as a mirror to the soul of the Wild West. It's a place where history and the supernatural converge, where the rugged individualism of the frontier meets the complexities of the human condition. It's a reminder that our world is filled with mysteries and wonders, and that sometimes, the past refuses to remain buried.

The De Soto Hotel continues to fascinate and terrify, a living testament to the enduring allure of the paranormal. It's more than just a building; it's a character in the rich tapestry of American folklore, a place where dreams and nightmares intertwine, where the boundaries between the earthly and the ethereal are fluid, and where the ghosts of the past still walk the halls, forever etched in the landscape of our collective imagination. In the De Soto, the Wild West lives on, its spirit undiminished, its legacy a haunting melody that continues to resonate, long after the last echoes have faded into the night.

The Crying Ghost of La Llorona in New Mexico

In the arid deserts and along the flowing rivers of New Mexico, a haunting cry echoes through the night. It's a sound that sends shivers down the spines of those who hear it, a lament that tells of a tragedy that transcends time and space. It is the cry of La Llorona, the Weeping Woman, a ghostly figure that has become an integral part of Hispanic folklore, particularly in the American Southwest.

The legend of La Llorona is as varied as the people who tell it, a story that has evolved and adapted to fit different times, places, and cultures. Yet, at its core, it is a tale of love, betrayal, and a mother's unbearable grief. In the most common version, La Llorona is a beautiful woman named Maria, who falls in love with a wealthy man and bears him two children. When he abandons her for another, in a fit of rage and despair, she drowns her children in a river. Realising the horror of her actions, she then drowns herself. Since that fateful day, her restless spirit wanders, weeping for her lost children, her cries a haunting reminder of her sorrow.

The legend of La Llorona has many iterations, each with its unique flavour and emphasis. In some versions, Maria is portrayed as a vain woman whose obsession with her beauty leads to her downfall. In others, she is a victim of circumstance, driven to madness by betrayal and loss. In certain retellings, La Llorona's haunting is localised to specific rivers or bodies of water, while in others, she is a more universal figure, her lament heard across vast landscapes. Some emphasise her role as a harbinger of doom, while others focus on her eternal search for redemption.

Through the years, countless individuals have claimed to have encountered La Llorona. Her spectral form is often seen near bodies of water, her white gown flowing, her face obscured by tears. The sound of her crying is said to be both mesmerising and terrifying, a sorrowful melody that resonates deep within the soul. In New Mexico, reported sightings have spanned centuries, from early Spanish settlers to modern-day residents. Her presence has been felt along the Rio Grande, in the arroyos of Santa Fe, and in the desolate plains of the desert. Some witnesses describe a feeling of intense sadness, a melancholy that lingers long after the encounter. Others speak of fear, of a chill that settles in the bones, a sense of dread that defies explanation.

The legend of La Llorona has transcended folklore to become a cultural symbol, reflecting broader themes and values within Hispanic culture. She is seen as a cautionary figure, a warning against the perils of vanity, passion, and unchecked emotion. She also represents the complexity of motherhood, the intense love that can turn to madness, the grief that can consume and destroy. Her story is a reminder of the fragility of human nature, the thin line that separates sanity from insanity, love from obsession. The legend has found expression in various art forms, from literature to music to film. It's a narrative that continues to inspire and captivate, a myth that speaks to universal human emotions and experiences.

The story of La Llorona fits seamlessly into the tapestry of the Wild West, a time and place characterised by lawlessness, struggle, and the clash of cultures. Her tale echoes the hardships of frontier life, the harsh realities that shaped the people and the land. The image of La Llorona wandering the desert, a lone figure against the vastness of the wilderness, resonates with the loneliness and isolation that many faced in the Wild West. Her tragedy is a reflection of the broader tragedy of a land marked by conflict, change, and loss.

In our modern age, the legend of La Llorona continues to be a subject of fascination and study. Paranormal investigators have sought to document her presence, employing technology and scientific methods to understand the phenomenon. Psychologists and sociologists have explored the psychological underpinnings of the legend, delving into the collective subconscious, the ways in which myths and legends shape our perception of reality.

The crying ghost of La Llorona is more than just a spooky tale; it's a living part of Hispanic heritage, a story that continues to evolve, reflecting the hopes, fears, and values of a people. Her haunting cry is a reminder that the past is never truly gone, that the pain and sorrow of a moment can echo through the ages. It's a call to remember, to reflect, and to recognize the power of storytelling, the ways in which legends and myths shape our understanding of ourselves and our place in the world.

Bigfoot of the Rockies: Myth or Reality?

The towering peaks and rugged wilderness of the Rocky Mountains have long been a place of mystery and intrigue, where legends thrive and tales of the unknown captivate the imagination. Among these stories, one stands out for its enduring fascination and widespread appeal: the legend of Bigfoot, a mysterious and elusive creature said to roam the vast forests and remote areas of the Rockies.

Known by various names such as Sasquatch, Yeti, or simply the "Wild Man of the Woods," Bigfoot has become an iconic figure in American folklore and a symbol of the untamed wilderness. Descriptions of the creature vary, but most agree that it is large, covered in thick hair, and walks upright like a human. Its footprints, often discovered in remote locations, are massive and distinct, giving the creature its name.

The legend of Bigfoot is not unique to the Rocky Mountains but has been reported across North America. However, the Rockies, with their vast and often inaccessible wilderness, have become a focal point for sightings and research. The area's history, steeped in the lore of the Wild West, adds a layer of mystique to the legend, blending the frontier spirit with the unknown.

Eyewitness accounts of Bigfoot in the Rockies are numerous and span generations. From hunters and hikers to park rangers and tourists, people from all walks of life have claimed to have seen the creature or evidence of its existence. These sightings are often accompanied by feelings of awe, fear, or a deep connection to nature. The experiences are profound and life-changing for some, leading them to dedicate their lives to understanding and proving the existence of Bigfoot.

Physical evidence, such as footprints, hair samples, and even purported photographs and videos, have been presented as proof of Bigfoot's existence. Researchers and enthusiasts have poured over this evidence, seeking to validate or debunk the claims. Scientific analysis has often been inconclusive, leaving room for interpretation and debate.

On the other side of the spectrum, there have been numerous hoaxes and deliberate attempts to deceive the public about Bigfoot. Some have crafted elaborate fake footprints, while others have donned costumes to impersonate the creature. These hoaxes have cast a shadow of doubt over genuine sightings and evidence, leading many to dismiss the legend as mere fantasy.

The cultural significance of Bigfoot in the Rockies and beyond is immense. It has inspired countless books, documentaries, films, and even festivals dedicated to the creature. It represents a longing for mystery, a desire to believe in something beyond our understanding. It's a reminder of the wild and untamed nature that still exists, hidden just beyond our reach.

But beyond the entertainment and mystique, the legend of Bigfoot raises essential questions about our relationship with the natural world. It challenges our understanding of what is possible and forces us to confront our own biases and beliefs. In a world increasingly dominated by technology and urbanisation, Bigfoot symbolises a longing for a connection to something primal and authentic.

The existence of Bigfoot in the Rockies remains an open question, with passionate arguments on both sides. Sceptics point to the lack of definitive evidence and the prevalence of hoaxes as proof that the legend is nothing more than a myth. Believers, on the other hand, see the creature as a living, breathing entity, a part of our natural world that remains elusive and misunderstood.

In the end, the legend of Bigfoot transcends the debate about its existence. It's a story that resonates with our deepest fears and desires, a tale that reflects our collective consciousness. Whether myth or reality, Bigfoot's shadow looms large over the Rockies, a symbol of the wild and mysterious, a challenge to our understanding of the world, and a reminder that some things, no matter how much we search, may remain forever beyond our grasp.

The Bigfoot of the Rockies continues to captivate and inspire, a paradox that embodies the spirit of the Wild West. It stands as a testament to the power of folklore and the human imagination, a legend that continues to evolve, reflecting our hopes, fears, and endless fascination with the unknown. It's a story that, like the towering peaks of the Rockies themselves, rises above the ordinary and touches something profound within us all.

The Specter of Hangman's Bridge: Justice or Vengeance?

Hidden in the shadowed valleys of Colorado's rugged terrain, Hangman's Bridge spans the dark waters of the Gunnison River, a lingering testament to the unforgiving nature of frontier justice. Its timeworn beams and creaking planks echo with the whispers of the past, a haunting melody that resonates through the lonely canyons.

Hangman's Bridge is more than just a crossing; it's a place where the spectral and the corporeal intertwine, where the cries of the wrongfully hanged are said to merge with the wind, giving voice to the restless spirits that seek either justice or revenge. Its very name conjures images of stern-faced vigilantes and desperate criminals, of life and death struggles played out on the precipice of eternity.

The most chilling tale associated with Hangman's Bridge is the haunting of a young miner, unjustly accused of stealing gold from his fellow prospectors. Despite his tearful protestations of innocence, he was dragged to the bridge and hung from its sturdiest beam. On moonlit nights, travellers have reported seeing his spectral figure, his lifeless eyes staring into the abyss, forever searching for the justice that eluded him in life. The wind through the canyon seems to carry his mournful cries, a haunting lament that chills the soul.

Others tell of a notorious outlaw, hanged for crimes he undoubtedly committed, whose dark spirit still prowls the vicinity of the bridge. His ghost is said to be vengeful, filled with a fury that transcends death. Locals speak in hushed tones of encounters with this menacing spectre, a shadowy figure who chases intruders from the bridge, his ghostly footsteps echoing on the wooden planks, his malevolent laughter reverberating through the night.

The lore of Hangman's Bridge reaches back to the earliest days of Colorado's wild frontier, when the gold rush brought men and women from all walks of life, driven by dreams of wealth and a new beginning. It was a time of great promise but also of great peril. Law and order were often makeshift affairs, meted out by self-appointed judges and juries that answered to no higher authority.

Justice was a concept in flux, shaped by the needs and desires of a community forging its existence in an untamed land. Those accused of crimes had little in the way of legal protection. Trials were hasty, verdicts swift, and punishments severe. In this environment, Hangman's Bridge became a symbol of the harsh code that governed life and death on the frontier.

But the bridge's haunted history is not confined to the spectral figures of the hanged. Other ghosts are said to inhabit this foreboding place, each with a story to tell, each bound to the bridge by the tragic circumstances of their demise. There are tales of a lovesick maiden who threw herself from the bridge after being spurned by her lover, her ghostly sobs heard on still nights when the river runs low. There are whispers of a phantom stagecoach that rumbles across the bridge, driven by a spectral coachman whose face is hidden beneath a tattered hat.

Paranormal investigators who have ventured to Hangman's Bridge have come away with evidence that defies easy explanation. Photographs have captured strange mists and unexplained lights. Audio recordings have revealed voices where no one was speaking, the words sometimes clear, sometimes garbled, but always tinged with an otherworldly quality. Even those sceptical of the supernatural have found themselves unnerved by the inexplicable occurrences that seem to plague this cursed crossing.

As the years have passed, the legends of Hangman's Bridge have become an integral part of Colorado's cultural fabric, passed down from generation to generation. They are tales that captivate and frighten, that speak to the primal fears that dwell within us all. They remind us that the past is never truly gone, that it lingers in the shadows, waiting for the moment when it can reach out and touch us once again.

The haunting of Hangman's Bridge is a rich tapestry of history and myth, of human frailty and the relentless march of time. It is a place where the boundary between the living and the dead seems porous, where the echoes of the past resonate with a clarity that transcends the ordinary.

In examining the spectral mysteries of Hangman's Bridge, we are confronted with questions that probe the very nature of existence. What does it mean to be guilty or innocent? How do we reconcile our longing for justice with our capacity for vengeance? What binds a soul to a place, and what might set it free?

These questions hang heavy over Hangman's Bridge, as weighty as the noose that once swung from its beams. They are questions without easy answers, complex riddles that continue to puzzle and intrigue those who dare to explore the haunted landscape of the Wild West.

If you find yourself near the Gunnison River on a cold and moonless night, you may wish to avoid the old crossing known as Hangman's Bridge. For within its weathered timbers and beneath its shadowed arches lies a mystery as profound as death itself, a haunting that continues to unfold, and a spectre that swings from the noose, forever etched in the annals of the paranormal phenomena of the Wild West.

Yet, for those who seek to understand the hidden recesses

of the human heart, who are drawn to places where the veil between worlds is thin, Hangman's Bridge offers a journey into the unknown. It is a gateway to a realm where fact and fiction blur, where the cries of the damned reverberate through time, and where the quest for justice may be an eternal struggle waged in the shadows of our darkest fears.

Hangman's Bridge stands as a silent sentinel to a bygone era, its wooden planks bearing the weight of history, its ghostly inhabitants a reminder of the complexity of the human condition. It is a place of mystery and wonder, a place where the living can commune with the dead, and where the lessons of the past are etched into the very fabric of the landscape.

The spectre of Hangman's Bridge continues to haunt the imagination, a chilling symbol of justice and vengeance, a place where the echoes of the past are never silent, and where the restless spirits of the Wild West still roam, tethered to the earth by unfulfilled desires and unquenchable thirsts. It is a place of legend and lore, a place where the dead speak, and where the living listen, ever watchful for the moment when the spectral figure of the hanged man swings once again from the noose, a ghostly reminder of a time and place that continue to resonate in the collective consciousness of a nation.

UFOs over Aurora: The 1897 Crash

In the small town of Aurora, Texas, lies a mystery as profound and perplexing as any in the annals of the Wild West. It's a tale that intertwines the human experience with the unexplainable, a story that challenges our understanding of reality itself. For within the quiet confines of this sleepy community, something extraordinary occurred in the late 19th century, something that continues to ignite curiosity and spark debate.

The date was April 17, 1897, a day that began like any other in the farming community of Aurora. The morning sun cast a golden glow over the fields, and the townsfolk went about their business, oblivious to the extraordinary event that was about to unfold.

As the day wore on, reports began to filter into town of a strange object in the sky. Eyewitnesses described it as a cigar-shaped craft, emitting a bright light and trailing smoke as it soared through the air. Its appearance was unlike anything the people of Aurora had ever seen, and its flight seemed to defy the known laws of physics.

The craft's erratic path led it over the town, where it was seen by numerous residents. Its movements were studied, its appearance analysed, but its origin remained a mystery. It seemed to be neither bird nor plane, neither man-made nor a natural phenomenon. It was an enigma, a puzzle that defied explanation.

Then, with a deafening crash, the object plummeted to the ground, striking a windmill on the property of a local judge, J.S. Proctor. The explosion that followed was heard for miles, and the debris scattered across the landscape, leaving a trail of destruction in its wake.

But the wreckage was not the only thing found at the crash site. Among the twisted metal and scorched earth lay the body of a being, unlike anything the townsfolk had ever seen. It was small in stature, with a frail frame and features that were distinctly non-human.

The discovery sent shockwaves through the community, sparking fear, curiosity, and endless speculation. Was this being from another world? Had Aurora been visited by extraterrestrial life? The questions were as numerous as they were unanswerable, and the mystery deepened with each passing day.

In the aftermath of the crash, the town's residents did what they felt was right. The alien being was given a Christian burial in the local cemetery, its grave marked with a simple stone. The wreckage was gathered and hidden away, its secrets locked behind closed doors.

Newspaper articles from the time document the incident in vivid detail, their accounts tinged with a mixture of awe and disbelief. They tell a story that is both fantastical and unnerving, a story that challenges our understanding of the world and our place in it.

As the years have passed, the tale of the Aurora crash has

become a part of UFO lore, a story that continues to captivate and intrigue. Modern-day researchers have delved into the archives, unearthing documents, interviewing descendants of the eyewitnesses, and conducting on-site investigations in an attempt to unravel the mystery.

Some have dismissed the incident as a hoax, a fabrication designed to put Aurora on the map. Others see in it evidence of a government cover-up, a deliberate attempt to hide the truth from the public. Still, others believe that the Aurora crash offers a glimpse into a reality that is broader and more complex than we can imagine, a reality that includes the possibility of life beyond our planet.

Despite the myriad theories and interpretations, the truth of the Aurora crash remains elusive. The physical evidence has been lost to time, the witnesses have passed away, and the grave of the alien being has been exhumed and found empty, its contents a mystery.

Yet the story endures, a haunting reminder of the unknown that lies just beyond our grasp. It is a tale that speaks to the human condition, to our longing for knowledge and our fear of the inexplicable. It is a story that resonates with the timeless themes of the Wild West, where the frontier was not just a physical place but a boundary between the known and the unknown, a gateway to a realm that defies comprehension.

The 1897 UFO crash in Aurora, Texas, stands as a testament to the complexity of our existence, a symbol of our quest for understanding, and a beacon that draws us ever onward in our exploration of the universe. It is a mystery that continues to unfold, a riddle that refuses to be solved, and a part of the rich tapestry of paranormal phenomena that have shaped our understanding of ourselves and our world.

As we gaze into the night sky, pondering the vastness of space and the possibility of life on other planets, we are reminded of the Aurora crash and the questions it has raised. We are called to look beyond the familiar, to embrace the unknown, and to acknowledge that the universe is a place of wonder and mystery, where the answers we seek may be as elusive and enigmatic as the UFOs over Aurora.

Legends of the Lake: The Spirits of Pyramid Lake

Pyramid Lake, nestled within the high desert of Nevada, is a place where the natural world meets the supernatural, where legends come to life, and where the boundaries between the earthly and the ethereal are blurred. This strikingly beautiful lake, named for the pyramid-like formations that rise from its depths, has long been a place of spiritual significance, not only for the native Paiute people but also for those drawn to its mystical allure.

The lake's deep, clear waters and the arid landscape that surrounds it create a setting that is both tranquil and foreboding. For the Paiute, the lake is a sacred place, a repository of their history, their beliefs, and their connection to the land. The legends that permeate the area are not mere stories but living embodiments of their culture and their understanding of the world.

One of the most enduring legends of Pyramid Lake is that of the Water Babies, otherworldly creatures said to inhabit the lake's depths. Descriptions of these beings vary, but they are often depicted as small, misshapen figures with a haunting cry that echoes across the water. The legend tells of a time when the Paiute would dispose of deformed or sickly infants in the lake, a practice born of necessity and survival. These lost souls are said to have transformed into the Water Babies, forever bound to the place of their demise.

The story is a tragic one, a reflection of the harsh realities of life in an unforgiving landscape. But it is also a tale that speaks to deeper truths, to the connection between the natural and the supernatural, and to the power of belief to shape our understanding of the world.

But the Water Babies are not the only spirits said to inhabit Pyramid Lake. There are tales of ghostly warriors and spectral maidens, of mysterious lights that dance across the water, and of eerie voices that whisper in the wind. These stories are not confined to the distant past but are part of the living folklore of the area, passed down through generations and kept alive by those who have experienced the unexplainable.

Modern-day sightings of strange phenomena at Pyramid Lake continue to fuel the legends. Fishermen speak of unexplained disturbances in the water, of feeling a presence that is both unsettling and inexplicable. Visitors tell of seeing figures that vanish upon closer inspection, of hearing cries that have no source, and of a sense of awe and wonder that defies description.

The spiritual significance of Pyramid Lake extends beyond the legends and the sightings. It is a place of ceremony and ritual, of prayer and meditation. The native Paiute hold the lake in reverence, recognizing it as a source of life and a gateway to the spiritual world. The natural formations that dot the landscape are not mere geological features but symbols of their cosmology, tangible manifestations of their beliefs.

For those drawn to the lake's mystical allure, Pyramid Lake

offers a connection to something greater, a pathway to understanding that transcends the physical world. Whether through Native American spirituality or New Age exploration, the lake is a place of discovery, a place where the mind and the spirit can commune with the unknown.

Researchers and paranormal investigators have also been drawn to Pyramid Lake, seeking to unravel its mysteries and to validate the experiences of those who have encountered the inexplicable. Their findings are often inconclusive, caught between science and belief, evidence and interpretation. But their efforts are a testament to the enduring fascination with the lake and the questions it raises.

Pyramid Lake stands as a singular point in the vast landscape of the Wild West, a place where legends are born and where the supernatural is part of the fabric of life. It is a place that challenges our understanding of the world, that calls us to look beyond the surface, and that reminds us that the unknown is not something to be feared but something to be explored.

It is a place where the spirits of the lake are not mere figments of the imagination but living entities that reach out to us, that beckon us to listen, to learn, and to embrace the mysteries of existence. It is a place where the natural and the supernatural converge, where the past mingles with the present, and where the earthly and the ethereal are forever intertwined.

In exploring the legends of Pyramid Lake, we delve into the heart of the Wild West, uncovering layers of history, myth, and symbolism. We encounter a world where reality blends with fantasy, where the stark realities of survival give way to the endless possibilities of the imagination.

We are left to ponder the nature of the supernatural and why certain places become imbued with spiritual significance. Is it merely the product of human psychology, our need to make sense of the unexplainable, or is there something more profound at work? Do the spirits of Pyramid Lake still wander, restless and unbound, a testament to the human spirit's indomitable will?

Pyramid Lake continues to fascinate and inspire, a place

where the legends of the Wild West come to life in the most unexpected ways. It serves as a reminder that our world is full of mysteries, waiting to be explored, and that the ghosts of the past may still walk among us, whispering secrets in the wind, forever etched in the landscape of our dreams and our fears.

Afterword

As I sit down to pen this afterword, the echoes of ghostly apparitions, spectral cowboys, haunting melodies, and unexplained phenomena linger in my mind. The journey through the vast and rugged terrains of the Wild West, exploring the depths of the supernatural and the unknown, has been both thrilling and enlightening. It's been an adventure that has connected me with the past, challenged my perceptions, and opened my eyes to the mysteries that lie just beyond the veil of reality.

The tales that fill the pages of "Spirits of the Frontier: True Tales of the Paranormal in the Wild West" are more than mere folklore or legends passed down through generations. They are windows into our history, our culture, and our very humanity. Through the investigation of these supernatural phenomena, I've delved into the timeless human yearning to understand the unknown, and I hope that, as readers, you have joined me in this exciting exploration.

Whether it's the enigmatic ghost lights of Marfa, Texas, the haunting melodies of the Ghost Dancer, the tragic cry of La Llorona in New Mexico, or the sacred energy of Devil's Tower in Wyoming, each chapter has revealed layers of complexity, tradition, fear, and wonder. These stories remind us that the supernatural is not confined to dark corners or hidden places; it is interwoven with our daily lives, our landscapes, and our collective psyche.

The Wild West has always been a place of rugged beauty and untamed nature, but as I've discovered, it's also a place teeming with paranormal activity. The spectral figures that haunt old mining towns, the mysterious creatures that roam the mountains, and the inexplicable occurrences that defy reason are all part of the rich tapestry that makes this region so intriguing. They are pieces of a puzzle that may never be fully solved but continue to captivate and inspire.

Being a paranormal investigator, I'm often asked if I truly believe in ghosts, cryptids, or extraterrestrial beings. My response is always the same: belief is a complex matter, often personal and deeply rooted in our individual experiences and perspectives. What I do believe in, wholeheartedly, is the importance of asking questions, seeking answers, and keeping an open mind.

The stories contained within this book are a testament to the enduring fascination with the unknown. They reflect a universal curiosity that transcends time, place, and culture. They challenge us to look beyond the surface, to question our assumptions, and to consider the possibilities that lie just out of reach.

My journey through the supernatural Wild West has been a reminder that the world is full of wonders waiting to be explored, and that the quest for understanding is a path we can all walk together. As you close this book, I invite you to carry these stories with you, to ponder the mysteries they present, and to continue the exploration in your own way.

The Wild West may be a place of history, but its spirits are very much alive. They beckon us to listen, to learn, and to embrace the unknown. May we always have the courage to answer their call.

Thank you for accompanying me on this incredible journey.

With gratitude,

Lee Brickley

About the Author

Lee Brickley is an investigator and author with more than 30 titles currently in publication covering a broad range of subjects including true crime, ancient history, the paranormal, and more.

Born in England, Brickley has been a professional writer for more than two decades. He regularly features in the media due to wide interest in his work, and he has made numerous TV appearances.

For more books in this series, simply search "Lee Brickley" on Amazon!